By May Nakamura
Illustrated by Natalie Kwee

Ready-to-Read

SIMON SPOTLIGHT
An imprint of Simon & Schuster Children's Publishing Division • 1230 Avenue of the Americas, New York, New York 10020
This Simon Spotlight edition May 2019 • SIMON SPOTLIGHT, READY-TO-READ, and colophon are registered trademarks of Simon & Schuster, Inc. For information about special discounts for bulk purchases, please contact Simon & Schuster Special Sales at 1-866-506-1949 or business@simonandschuster.com.
Manufactured in the United States of America 0319 LAK • 2 4 6 8 10 9 7 5 3 1 • Library of Congress Cataloging-in-Publication Data • Names: Nakamura, May, author. | Kwee, Natalie, illustrator. Title: If you love dolphins, you could be ... / by May Nakamura ; illustrated by Natalie Kwee. Description: New York : Simon Spotlight, 2019. | Series: If you love | Audience: Age 5-7. | Identifiers: LCCN 2019005403 | ISBN 9781534444683 (pbk : alk. paper) | ISBN 9781534444690 (hc : alk. paper) | ISBN 9781534444706 (eBook) • Subjects: LCSH: Marine animals—Vocational guidance—Juvenile literature. | Aquatic animals—Health—Juvenile literature. | Aquatic biologists—Vocational guidance—Juvenile literature. | Underwater cinematography—Vocational guidance—Juvenile literature. Classification: LCC QL122.2 N26 2019 | DDC 591.77023—dc23 LC record available at https://lccn.loc.gov/2019005403

Glossary

Aquarium: a tank of water used as a home for fish and marine animals, or a building with many of these tanks that people can visit to learn about marine animals

Aquatic veterinarian: a doctor who takes care of marine animals at zoos, aquariums, or animal hospitals

Beach cleanup: an event where people clean garbage and waste from the beach to help protect it

Checkup: a physical exam performed by a doctor to make sure a person or an animal is healthy

Ecosystem: a community made up of plants and animals in a specific environment

Marine biologist: a scientist who studies plants and animals that live in the ocean

Microscope: a scientific instrument with a lens that makes very small objects appear much larger

Scuba dive: to swim underwater using special equipment that lets you breathe through a tube and mask connected to an oxygen tank

Underwater filmmaker: a person who films life underwater using special video cameras and breathing equipment

X-ray: a procedure that allows doctors to see the inside of a person's or an animal's body

Note to readers: Some of these words may have more than one definition. The definitions above are how these words are used in this book.

CONTENTS

Introduction

Do you love dolphins
and other marine animals?
Do you enjoy going to the beach
and visiting aquariums?

Did you know that some people get to spend time with dolphins every day as part of their jobs? When you grow up, you could work with marine animals too!

Chapter 1: Aquatic Veterinarian

Have you ever taken a pet to the doctor?
Dolphins and other marine animals need doctors too. A doctor who works with dolphins is called an aquatic veterinarian (say: uh-KWA-tick veh-tuh-ruh-NAIR-ian).

Many people with this job
work at zoos, aquariums,
or animal hospitals.
They help keep animals healthy.

They are often in charge of deciding what the marine animals eat. Just like humans, animals need healthy, balanced meals.

They may examine the mouth of a pufferfish or listen to a sea turtle's heartbeat and lungs!

They take care of sick or hurt animals too, and decide if medicine or surgery is needed. If a sea lion has trouble swimming, they may do an X-ray to look at its bones.

Aquatic veterinarians take care
of all kinds of animals
with different needs.
When a beluga whale is having
a baby, the doctors do tests to
make sure everything is on track.

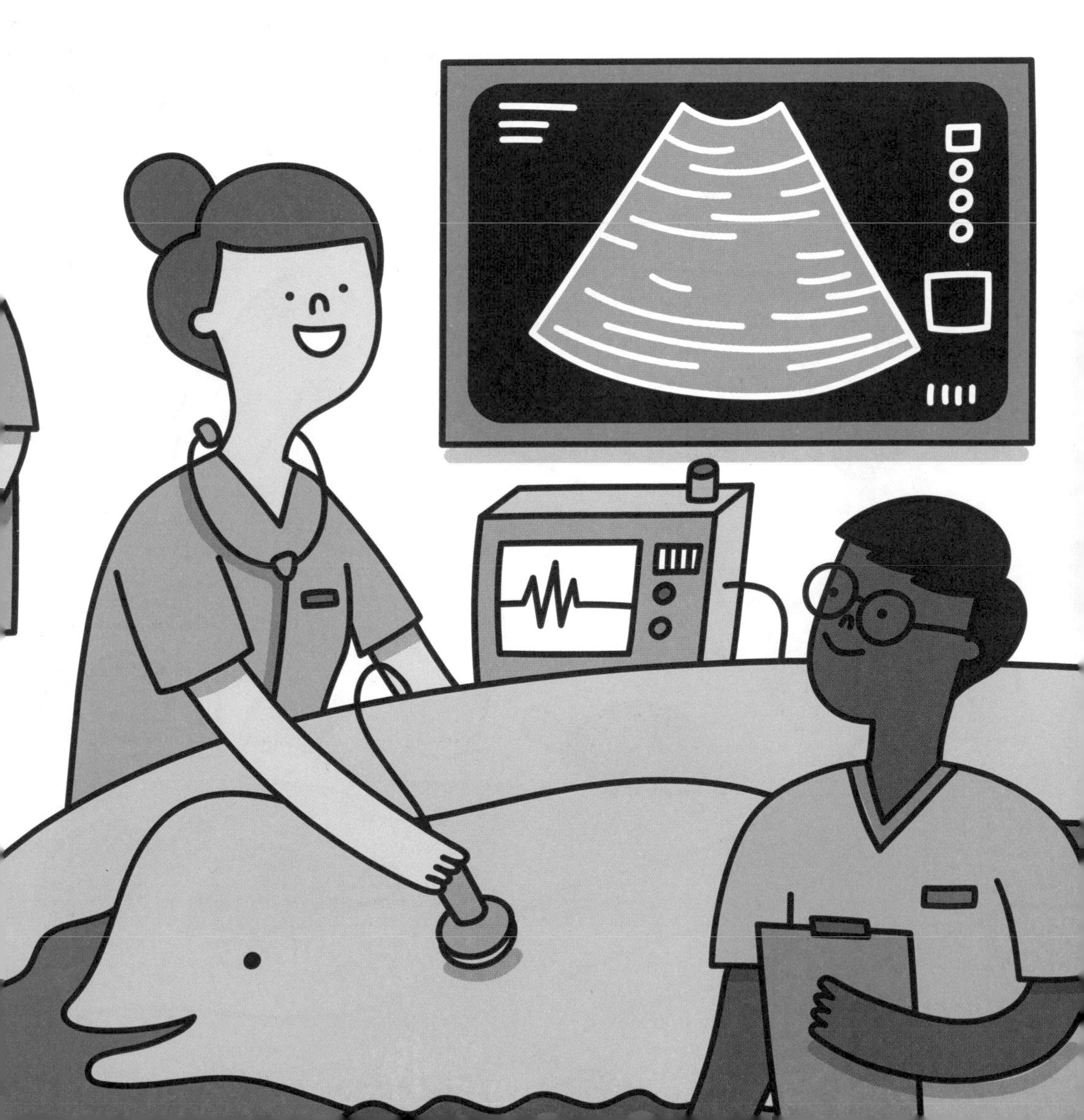

When there is an oil spill or another disaster, they help clean and care for wild animals too. It takes a lot of problem-solving to figure out how to help, but it feels great to help sick animals get better again!

If you want to be an aquatic veterinarian, you can learn about different marine animals at an aquarium.
Maybe someday you will help care for them too!

Chapter 2: Marine Biologist

There are also scientists who study animals and plants that live in the ocean.
They are called marine biologists (say: muh-REEN bye-ALL-o-jists).

There are many different types of marine biologists, but they all have one thing in common: they want to conserve, or protect, the ocean.

The ocean has many ecosystems (say: EE-ko-sis-tums).
An ecosystem is a community made up of plants, animals, and the area around them.

Today the ocean has many problems. The ocean water is getting warmer, making it hard for these plants and animals to stay alive.

Marine biologists study the ocean and its ecosystems so they can learn how to help. Some days they might use a microscope to study the smallest sea creatures.

Other days they might track dolphins in the wild and watch how they behave.

They might even dive underwater to collect samples!

Marine biologists also study what happens when people catch too many of one kind of fish. This puts the fish at risk of dying out and hurts animals that rely on that fish for food. Scientists and governments are trying to help.

You do not have to be a marine biologist to help protect the ocean. One thing you can do now, with your parent or guardian, is attend a beach cleanup event.

You can pick up trash and plastics on the shore to keep them from washing into the water.
You might even meet a marine biologist who is helping out!

Chapter 3: Underwater Filmmaker

Do you like watching TV shows and movies about the ocean? Whenever you see videos of dolphins, ruins, or a sunken ship, those videos were probably taken by an underwater filmmaker.

In order to take videos, underwater filmmakers must know how to scuba dive.
They need to be strong swimmers and be able to hold their video cameras steady!
They use a special video camera that works underwater.

An underwater filmmaker also needs to be patient.
It can take a long time for an animal to swim by or for filmmakers to get the shot that they want.
Luckily, the beautiful view makes it worth the wait!

Even so, filmmakers try not to get too close.
They never want to hurt or scare the animals.

Thanks to underwater filmmakers, people all around the world can learn about the ocean and see amazing videos of it.
People use the videos to study how animals behave in the wild.

If you want to be an underwater filmmaker, you can practice taking your own videos on land.
You can also learn how to swim with help from your parent, guardian, or a swim coach.
And one day you might get to make a movie all about dolphins!

The ocean is a big place.
There are still so many things
that we can learn about it.
Some say that most of it
has not yet been explored!